THE ESSENTIAL HAND & FOOT

THE ESSENTIAL HAND & FOOT

HARRY WASTRACK

DEDICATION

For my mother, Norma, who may very well be the best overall
Hand & Foot player any of us will ever meet.

To order additional copies of this book, contact:
Xlibris Corporation
1-888-795-4274
www.Xlibris.com
Orders@Xlibris.com
28535

Contents

Introduction to Hand & Foot

An Addictive New Card Game

"So what is it with that game that you get so into it?" That is the question asked most often by people who have never played Hand & Foot of their friends and relatives who do. Allow me to respond.

I have always enjoyed playing cards, both as a verb and as a noun. That is, I eagerly learn and play new card games, and I avidly collect old decks of cards. My friends and family know this, which brings us to 1997. A friend invited my wife and me over to teach us a card game that she thought we might like, called **Hand & Foot**. No one realized at the time that our friend was creating a monster.

In the late 1940s and early 1950s, Canasta was all the rage. Perfectly suited to the times, Canasta was not generally considered a gambling game, but it was just as competitive and entertaining as poker. Though not as complicated and intense as contract bridge, it was also not a child's game, like Old Maid, or a grandma's game, like Chinese Checkers. It was a card game with an attitude more akin to the board game Monopoly, which allowed people to socialize while playing and kept even quiet or shy people involved.

Fast forward 40 years or so. Canasta is still played, though mostly by people who learned the game more than a generation ago. However, somewhere (I do not know exactly where) someone (I do not know exactly who) decided that Canasta needed to have new life breathed into it, thus this new variation called Hand & Foot. Based on the little bit of information on Hand & Foot that I have been able to find, it probably started to evolve in the late 1980s or early 1990s. There are literally dozens of regional rule variations, but the fundamentals of the game remain more or less constant.

As it is with most new Hand & Foot players, I was subsequently to discover that it took only a quick practice hand to teach the gist of the game. Though it's similarities to Canasta are unmistakable, Hand & Foot is an edgier game that allows players to be more aggressive. Everyone has a strategy, some quite elaborate, others quite generic, but the caveat to each is "if the cards cooperate." The luck of the draw is a variable everyone has to take into account. Among Hand & Foot players there are often heard frustrated sighs and disgusted groans. There is also breathless anxiousness as players sweat out an opponent's turn hoping he will not go out before a Foot can be played or a red three can be discarded. Like a spirited game of Monopoly, Hand & Foot tends to bring out elements of personality heretofore unknown among its players, you know, sort of a playful viciousness.

It only takes one round of Hand & Foot for a new player to recognize the objectives and basic strategies, . . . and the opportunities for deviousness. Also, while a veteran player who plays a solid game has a definite advantage, a novice can have fun and even prevail. It cannot be taken for granted that the best and most experienced player at the table will win a game of Hand & Foot. The cards do not always allow that. And there is that adrenaline rush that comes from just barely pulling out a win. It is probably that adrenaline rush that makes the game so addictive. This is why someone who has just played his first game of Hand & Foot will invariably insist on right away playing a second—he thinks he has figured it out.

My wife and I greatly enjoyed that first evening of Hand & Foot. We have played it countless times since, both against just each other and on numerous social occasions. We have taught the game to most of our friends and family, who have in turn taught the game to their friends and families. (No one who visits my mother and her sister leaves their house without playing at least one game.)

Establishing the Rules

It did not take long for the people we had taught the game to ask where they could find a written copy of the rules, for themselves and for others they would like to teach. It seems that after two or three degrees of separation, the rules tend to become a bit convoluted. As I mentioned, Hand & Foot was new to me until 1997. I had never heard of it. However, as I also said, it is quite similar to Canasta. Therefore, I consulted my books of *Hoyle* and *Scarne on Cards* to see if it was one of the lesser known variations. There was no mention of a game called Hand & Foot in either, and none of the cited variations of Canasta—Samba, Boliva, Mexicana, Italian Canasta, Cuban Canasta, etc.—were in effect Hand & Foot by another name.

My efforts to research the game next took me to the Internet. I found perhaps a half dozen websites that mentioned Hand & Foot, but the descriptions of the game and its rules varied quite extensively. There are even at least two versions that use proprietary non-standard decks of cards. However, I was able to find no definitive authority on the game and no standard set of rules for it. In other words, Hand & Foot appears to be one of those evolving regional games that just begs for standardization.

To help out, based on what I was taught about the game, what I was able to glean from the Internet, and my knowledge of Canasta, I compiled and printed out five pages of rules. Much to my surprise, those five pages have been rather widely distributed, and my simply compiling the rules for Hand & Foot and committing them to paper has somehow made me an authority on the game.

Who Is Best?

In 1998, my wife came up with the idea of hosting a Hand & Foot Tournament. We had relatives coming to visit and a number of friends who loved to play the game. Wouldn't it be fun . . .

As it turned out, it was fun. That first year we had 17 people at four tables. Everyone played four games. The top two finishers at each table moved up to the next table for the next game, except for Table Number One, where the winners stayed while the losers were exiled to Table Number Four.

I would say that half the people playing in the tournament were in it for fun. The other half were in it for blood and determined to know who was the best. It was a day of lively banter, some gloating, and a lot of muttering and cursing. At the end of four games, the top four players—those who had beaten the most opponents throughout the tournament—played a championship round. You could have heard a pin drop—there was absolute silence while they played. When it was over, people held their breath while the final score was tallied.

Everyone chipped in on food and refreshments. My wife handed out trophies for first and last place. We were exhausted after almost 12 hours of card playing. And the one question everyone asked was "When is next year's tournament?"

One has been held each year since. I am pleased to somewhat immodestly report that I myself won the tournament in 2002.

A Governing Body

It was probably during conversation between games of the first tournament that my brother first brought up the idea of getting Hand & Foot officially recognized as a separate and distinct card game in the Book of Hoyle. Somewhere in that conversation, the idea of establishing an organized body to officially sanction the standard rules for Hand & Foot (since to the best of our knowledge no such organization exists) came up. Thus the North American Hand and Foot Society (NAHFS—pronounced na-HAF-ass) was born.

These, therefore, are my credentials for authoring this book— founding member of NAHFS, the 2002 National Hand & Foot Champion (as recognized by NAHFS), and the guy who once wrote down and printed out five pages of rules.

Standard Rules—
For Individual Players

Getting Set Up—What You Will Need

Players:

One of the most appealing aspects of Hand & Foot is that it can be played by any number from two to nine, though it does become a bit unwieldy with more than six players. With four, six, eight, or nine players there is the option of playing as teams, which will be discussed in later chapters.

One of the players should have a pencil and paper and be designated the **scorekeeper**. This task requires competency in the basic math skills of addition and subtraction. Some scorekeepers have been known to use calculators.

Cards, . . . and lots of them:

What distinguishes Hand & Foot from virtually every other card game is the number of cards involved—one deck of cards for every player in the game, plus one. That is, for two players, use three decks, for four players use five decks, etc. These are to be 54-card decks—the standard 52 cards plus two jokers each.

The cards are all shuffled together into one large multiple deck. When four or more players are involved, shuffling can become a group effort. (Try to imagine the combined ten decks needed for nine players!) Often it is easiest just to do the old Granny shuffle on the tabletop. Some groups even prefer to use automatic card shufflers.

There are also certain considerations to keep in mind when selecting the decks of cards that will be used. Playing cards come in two standard sizes—poker-sized (2 ½ inches by 3 ½ inches) and bridge-sized (2 ¼ inches by 3 ½ inches). It is generally easier to shuffle cards that are all the same size. It is also easier to accurately cut cards that are the same size, an aspect of the game that will be described shortly.

Also, if you intend to separate the cards back into individual decks after the game, the task becomes easier if each deck has a different back design or color. Some regular players even go so far as to number the decks with a magic marker.

Playing Surface:

A spacious playing area is required, as players will be laying down their cards to create melds. A typical dining room table can usually accommodate four to six players, but gets a bit cramped with seven or more.

Extras that make playing easier:

- A two-section **card tray**, like those used to play Canasta—one side to hold the cards not yet in play or "stock," one side to hold the discards.

- **Cardholders**—since players can wind up holding 20 or more cards at a time, which can be troublesome for smaller hands. There are a variety of types available, including the one pictured below. Cardholders are also simple enough to make if you happen to have a table saw that can cut a few grooves into a block of wood.

- A kitchen turntable or **Lazy Susan**, to hold the card tray and thus make it more accessible to the respective players when their turns come. For larger numbers of players at a big table, it comes in really handy. Following is a table, Hand & Foot game in progress, with a card tray, card holders, and a Lazy Susan all in place:

Playing the Game

The Deal:

Instead of the cards being dealt, in Hand & Foot, after the multiple decks are thoroughly shuffled together, each player attempts to cut exactly 22 cards off the top. Each player then proceeds to alternately divide the cards he has cut into two piles of 11 cards each. If a player has cut more than 22 cards, the excess is returned to the collective deck or "**stock**." If a player has cut less than 22 cards, additional cards as necessary are drawn from the stock. If a player has made a precise cut of 22 cards, that player scores 100 bonus points.

Each player keeps one pile of cards as his **Hand** and passes the other pile on to the next player, moving clockwise around the table, as that player's **Foot**. Thus, before play begins, each player should have an 11-card Hand and an 11-card Foot.

The Hand and the Foot:

Initially, the Foot is set aside and left face down, concealed to all, while the Hand is picked up and played until depleted. Only when the Hand is played and depleted can a player pick up and play the cards contained in the Foot—a player may not even look at the cards contained in his Foot until that time.

A player may play all the cards in his Hand, if able, then pick up the Foot and continue to play within the same turn. Otherwise a player must play all but one card in the Hand, discard the remaining card, and begin to play the Foot in the subsequent turn.

The Play:

One player is chosen by some mutually agreed upon method to begin play, then proceeding clockwise, each subsequent player takes a turn. (At the beginning of subsequent rounds, the player who begins play also rotates clockwise.)

The first player (for each round):

1. Draws two cards from the stock;

2. Melds cards if he can and wishes to;

3. Discards one card face-up to create the **"discard pile."** By discarding, the player signifies that he has completed the turn and may play no further (that is, lay down anymore cards into melds) until every other player around the table has also taken a turn.

Subsequent players:

1. Subsequent players have the option of also drawing two cards from the stock, or picking from the discard pile if they can and wish to. Each subsequent player may also meld cards as he can and wishes to, and will signify that he has completed his respective turn by discarding one card, adding to the discard pile;

2. Play continues, each player in turn, until one player **"goes out."** Unless he goes out, a player must always hold at least one card.

Object of the game:

The general object of play is to score points by starting **"melds"** of cards of the same rank and building them into **"books."** In each of four rounds, play ends when any player has melded all of the cards in his Hand, and all the cards in his Foot, to create at least the minimum required number of books, and has discarded one final card. **There must always be a discard to end a round.**

The winner of the game is the player who has accumulated the most total points of those playing over the course of four rounds.

Melding and Creating Books:

A meld consists of at least three cards of the same rank—or at least two cards of the same rank and one wildcard—laid face up on the table and spread out for all to see. A player may build only one meld of cards of each rank. A player adds cards of the same rank or wildcards to a meld until seven cards are accumulated, at which point the meld becomes a book. The cards are then stacked and squared up into a pile.

A natural meld (thus far) of Jacks

A dirty meld of sevens

There are two types of books—**"natural"** and mixed or **"dirty."** A natural book consists of at least seven cards of the same rank and includes no wildcards. A dirty book consists of at least seven cards of the same rank, but includes among those seven at least one wildcard as a substitute for a natural card. At all times natural cards must outnumber wildcards in a meld by at least one, thus at no time may more than three wildcards be used to create a dirty book. Additional natural cards of the same rank may be added to a completed book to increase the card count, but wildcards may not be added once a meld has become a book.

Each natural book earns 500 bonus points. Each dirty book earns 300 bonus points. A natural book is so designated by placing a red card (either a heart or a diamond) of that particular rank on top. A dirty book is similarly designated with a black card (either a spade or a club) of that particular rank (versus a wildcard).

Card values:

Each card has the following point value, which is calculated into initial meld count and scoring:

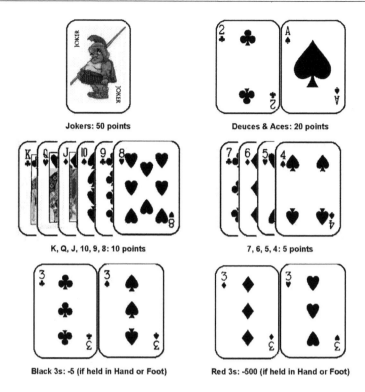

Jokers: 50 points

Deuces & Aces: 20 points

K, Q, J, 10, 9, 8: 10 points

7, 6, 5, 4: 5 points

Black 3s: -5 (if held in Hand or Foot)

Red 3s: -500 (if held in Hand or Foot)

Initial Meld:

The first time a player lays down cards to create a meld or melds, the cards used in those melds must meet the minimum card count requirement for that round. That is, the total point value of the melded cards must not be less than the designated minimum for that round. The initial meld requirement in each respective round must be met before a player can pick from the discard pile or pick up his Foot. Once the initial meld requirement for the round is met, a player may add to or create additional melds as he wishes, and may pick up his Foot when play allows. The following are the initial meld requirements for each round.

1st Round	60 points
2nd Round	90 points
3rd Round	120 points
4th Round	150 points

The initial meld consists of card count only. Bonus points from creating a book do not count toward an initial meld requirement. That is, a natural book of 4's counts only as 35 points toward the initial meld requirement. The bonus value for creating a book counts only in the tally at the end of the round.

An initial meld of 90 points:

4 fives @ 5 points each	=	20 points
3 nines @ 10 points each	=	30 points
2 deuces @ 20 points each	=	40 points
		90 points

35 points toward an initial meld:
(the 500 bonus points for a natural book cannot be applied toward the initial meld count)

7 fours @ 5 points each	=	35 points

Card uses:

Wildcards: All jokers and all deuces are wild and may be used to substitute for any card in a meld, however, the natural cards must always outnumber the wild cards in a meld by at least one. That is, a meld of three or four cards can include no more than one wildcard, a meld of five or six cards can include no more than two wildcards. No more than three wildcards may be used to complete a meld.

 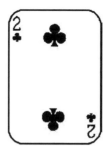

Black threes: Black threes cannot be melded, only discarded. Any black threes remaining in a player's Hand or Foot when another player goes out count as negative five points against the player holding them.

Red threes: Red threes cannot be melded, only discarded. Any red threes remaining in a player's Hand or Foot when another player goes out count as negative 500 points against the player holding them. (Yes, other players' strategies do include trying to catch you with red threes in your Hand or Foot!)

All other cards may be used to build melds and create books.

Picking from the Discard Pile:

When a player chooses to pick from the **discard pile** instead of drawing two cards from the stock:

1. The player picking from the discard pile must present at least two natural cards of the same rank as the top card on the discard pile from among the cards that he is holding. That is, cards that are currently in play, not cards that have already been melded, and not cards contained in the Foot if the player has not yet picked it up. Note: These must be two natural cards of the same rank as the top card of the discard pile, not one natural card and one wildcard. For instance, if the top card is a jack, you must lay down at least two jacks from among the cards you are holding to pick from the discard pile.

2. Any cards presented and the top card of the discard pile must be immediately melded. If it is the player's initial meld for the round, he must meet the initial meld count requirement for the round before continuing. Only the top card of the discard pile may be included in the initial meld count—no other cards in the discard pile may be used. If the player cannot thus meet the initial meld count requirement, the top card is returned to the discard pile and the player must draw two cards from the stock to conduct his turn.

3. If the player has met the requirements of Number 1 and Number 2 above, he must take the top seven cards from the discard

pile—the top card, which he has just matched with at least two from his Hand, plus the next six. If there are not at least seven cards in the discard pile, the player takes the entire pile. The player may not choose to pick less than seven cards if there are at least that many in the discard pile.

4. The player then conducts his turn as he normally would, melding cards as he can and wishes to, including those he has just obtained from the discard pile. As usual he concludes his turn by discarding one card.

Discards:

A player may discard any card he wishes. Any discard except threes or wildcards may be picked by the next player if that player can present two natural cards of the same rank from among the cards he is holding. Discarding a red three, a black three, or a wildcard essentially blocks the discard pile from being picked for one turn—the next player is not allowed to pick from the discard pile regardless of the cards that player holds.

Going Out:

A player is eligible to go out when he has at least one natural book and at least one dirty book. A player goes out by playing all the cards in his Hand and all the cards in his Foot. The player going out must have a discard. For going out, a player receives a bonus of 100 points.

Tallying the Score:

After one player has gone out, each player adds up his total bonus points:

Natural book	500 points each
Dirty book	300 points each
Perfect cut (22 cards)	100 points
Going out	100 points

Each player then adds up the total count for all melded cards, including those in completed books—50 points for each joker, 20 points for each ace and deuce, 10 points for each eight, nine, ten, jack, queen, or king, and 5 points for each four, five, six, or seven.

Each player, except the player who went out, must then add up the total count for any cards that remain in his Hand and/or Foot. The total count for these cards apply negatively against the player's score. Remember, each black three that remains in a player's Hand or Foot counts as negative five points when another player goes out, and each red three counts negative 500 points. (Yes, other players will try to go out before you have played your Foot and yes, a player's count can go negative.)

Scoring example: Player #1, having completed at least one natural book and at least one dirty book and having depleted all the cards in his Hand and all the cards in his Foot, has just discarded his last remaining card and has gone out. Prior to going out he had melded the following cards:

A natural book of fives -- 7 fives	7 fives @ 5 points = 35 points
A dirty book of jack's -- 4 jacks, 2 deuces, and 1 joker	4 Jacks @ 10 points = 40 points 2 two deuces @ 20 points = 40 points 1 joker @ 50 points = 50 points 130 points
A dirty book of tens – 5 tens and 3 deuces (1 ten was added after the book was completed)	5 tens @ 10 points = 50 points 3 deuces @ 20 points = 60 points 110 points
A meld of eights -- 4 eights	4 eights @ 10 points = 40 points
A meld of Aces -- 3 Aces	3 Aces @ 20 points = 60 points
A dirty meld of queens – 2 queens and 1 joker	2 queens @ 10 points = 20 points 1 joker @ 50 points = 50 points 70 points

Player #1's score:
   Bonus Points:
 	
   Total Card Count:
	(going out) 100 points
	(1 natural book of fives) 500 points
	(2 dirty books of jacks & tens) 600 points
	445 points

Score for Round:	1,645 points

Meanwhile, **Player #2,** who made a perfect cut of 22 at the start of the round, was not been able to deplete his Hand, and thus did not have a chance to play his Foot when Player #1 went out. Following are the cards that he has melded, as well as the cards still remaining in his Hand and his Foot:

A dirty book of sixes – 5 sixes and 2 deuces	5 sixes @ 5 points = 25 points 2 deuces @ 20 points = 40 points 65 points
A meld of fours – 3 fours	3 fours @ 5 points = 15 points
A dirty meld of kings – 3 kings and 1 deuce	3 kings @ 10 points = 30 points 1 deuce @ 20 points = 20 points 50 points
Cards remaining in Hand	1 Ace @ 20 points = 20 points 1 queen, 1 ten @ 10 points = 20 points 1 seven @ 5 points = 5 points 1 black three @ 5 points = 5 points 50 points
Unplayed Foot	2 Aces @ 20 points = 40 points 1 king, 1 jack, 1 ten, 2 nines @ 10 points = 50 points 1 six, 1 five, 1 four @ five points = 15 points 1 red three @ 500 points = 500 points 605 points

Player #2's score:
    Bonus Points:
 	
    Total Card Count:
	points (perfect cut of 22) 100 points
	(1 dirty book of sixes) 300 points
	(melded) 445 points
	(left in Hand, Foot) -655 points

Score for Round:	-125 points

Depleted Stock:

If no player goes out before the last card in the stock is drawn, when the last player able to draw cards discards, play ends, unless the next player is able and wishes to pick from the discard pile. If the next player does pick from the discard pile—the top seven cards—then plays those cards and discards, but does not go out, the subsequent player also has the option to pick from the discard pile if he can and wishes to, and so on. If no one has gone out, play concludes when the stock is depleted and the player whose turn is next either cannot or does not wish to pick from the discard pile.

If play ends because of a depleted stock, the cards each player holds at the end of play count against his or her point tally.

Standard Rules—For Partners

Following are the differences in the rules to Hand & Foot as pertains to play with partners.

Players:

With partnerships Hand & Foot can be played by four (two teams of two players), six (three teams of two players or two teams of three players), eight (four teams of two players), or nine (three teams of three players) players. Four players to a team is really not viable. More than nine players should be broken down into at least two separate games.

The partners must be evenly distributed around the table.

With four players—Teams A & B, two players each—the players should be seated alternately A-B-A-B:

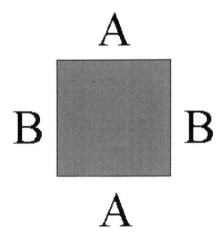

With six players—Teams A, B & C, two players each—the players should be seated A-B-C-A-B-C:

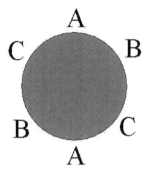

With six players—Teams A & B, three players each—the players should be seated A-B-A-B-A-B:

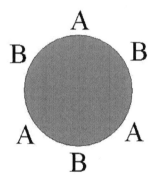

With eight players—Teams A, B, C & D, two players each—the players should be seated A-B-C-D-A-B-C-D:

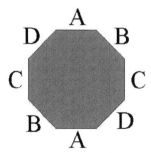

With nine players—Teams A, B & C, three players each—the players should be seated A-B-C-A-B-C-A-B-C:

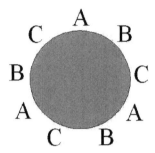

Playing Surface:

Surprisingly, less space is needed than if everyone is playing individually, as only one partner will keep the melds for each team.

The Deal:

Each player attempts to cut exactly 22 cards to divide into a Hand and a Foot and each player can score 100 bonus points for his team if he does.

Melding and Creating Books:

The rules for melding and creating books remain the same, except teams are allowed to create multiple books of the same rank. That is, once a team has a book, natural or dirty, of jacks, they can again be melded with the intention of creating another book of jacks.

However, only one meld of cards of a particular rank can be built at a time. A team cannot have a natural meld of sevens and a dirty meld of sevens being built simultaneously.

Initial Meld:

The minimum initial meld requirements remain the same as for individual play, however, it falls to one partner to come up with the entire initial meld count for his team in each round. It does not matter which partner. After that, each partner may create or add to the melds of his team. (In the latter rounds of a game, a team can, and often does, find itself in the frustrating position of not having a team member who can come up with the 120 or 150 points needed for the initial meld and thus is locked out of play until one does.)

Going out:

A team of two partners is eligible to go out when it has accumulated at least two natural books and at least three dirty books. A team of three partners is eligible to go out when it has accumulated at least three natural books and at least four dirty books.

Once a team has accumulated the minimum number of completed books to go out, any of the partners on the team may go out on behalf of his team. That partner may seek permission from his partner(s) by asking, "May I go out?" The partner(s) may respond only by saying "Yes" or "No." The responding partner(s) may not pass along any other information. At that point, the partner who asked either may or may not go out—it is his decision. He is not bound by a partner's response.

As in individual play, the player going out on behalf of his team must have a discard, and for going out, the team receives a bonus of 100 points.

Tallying the score:

As in individual play, the cards that remain in a player's Hand and Foot count negatively against his team when someone else has gone out. This includes the cards held by the partner(s) of the player who has gone out. It can happen that one partner goes out before the other partner has played his Foot. The wisdom of doing this is discussed in the Strategies for Partners section of this book.

It is not uncommon for final scores after four rounds of partnership play to reach 10,000 points or more.

What to Discard

What to discard is the first and most frequent decision a Hand & Foot player must make. Usually making the decision is relatively uncomplicated and straight forward. However, at certain points in the game and in certain situations, discarding the right card can make all the difference as to whether a player loses or wins, or at least has a chance to win.

Following is some guidance on things to keep in mind when discarding.

1. **Red threes.** Under the standard rules of Hand & Foot, it is difficult to imagine a situation in which the first card you would choose to discard is something other than a red three, if indeed you are holding a red three. There is no downside to getting rid of it. There is no upside to keeping it.

2. **Black threes.** Black threes are the next easiest choice for a discard. Though a black three is only negative five points if you are caught with one in your Hand when someone else goes out, you yourself cannot get to your Foot or go out until you have discarded it.

   However, there is a strategy that has players acquiring and holding onto black threes as safe discards, since they cannot be picked from the discard pile. Consider doing this if protecting the discard pile is of importance to you.

3. **Wildcards.** A wildcard is usually discarded only out of desperation.

   • A wildcard, like a red or black three, blocks the next player from picking from the discard pile. If that absolutely has to be prevented, a wildcard is a safe discard.

- As can happen on occasion, a player just holds too many wildcards and cannot play them all. Discarding it is a way to get rid of one.

- Sometimes, toward the end of a round, a player plays all the cards that he can, but cannot go out. He may wind up holding two wildcards or a wildcard and another card that is needed to build a natural book. At such times, a wildcard is the logical discard.

- Also toward the end of a round, a player may need to deplete the cards he is holding of as much count as he can because he expects his opponent will go out. That would be the time to throw away a joker (and its 50-point count) if it cannot be played.

- Note: One aspect of discarding a wildcard that must always be considered is that a discard pile with a wildcard among the top seven cards is quite desirable. If you want to tempt an opponent to pick from the discard pile in a subsequent turn, throwing a wildcard onto it is probably the best way to do that.

4. **Everything else.** After red threes, black threes, and wildcards, any other discard is fair game for an opponent to pick. Before throwing away any other card, there are two questions to ask yourself: a) Do you *care* if your opponent picks from the discard pile? And if yes, b) Do you *want* your opponent to pick from the discard pile?

- Early in a round, what to discard is really a no-brainer. Discard what you want to get rid of, the misfits. Usually at the start of a round, everyone is just disposing of threes and the discard pile is not that attractive anyway. Also, if it is the third or fourth round of the game, it is not likely that people yet have the card count for the initial meld they need to pick from the discard pile. However, as the round progresses and the various players have drawn cards from the stock three or four times, they have accumulated several pairs, as well as the card count for their initial melds. What do you discard then?

Unless your opponent has melded, the only thing you can base your decision on is what your opponent has discarded. Chances are he is still just getting rid of misfits himself, which makes whatever he throws away as safe a discard as anything. Otherwise, just continue to throw your own misfits, because there is really nothing else you can do.

Note, however, that when Hand & Foot players are trying to build up card count for an initial meld, they tend to discard their 5-counts—fours, fives, sixes, and sevens—while holding onto their higher count misfits in the hope of pairing them up. If you already have the initial meld count, you may want to hang onto those 5-counts in order to steal a pile.

• Once your opponent has started to meld his cards, you can start to make judgements as to what are safe discards. Still you likely must ask yourself which is more important—preventing your opponent from picking from the discard pile, or getting rid of your own misfits regardless of what your opponent might do?

If you have decided that you must get rid of your own misfits, then throw what you may. However, if you really want to protect the discard pile, look at what and how your opponent has melded. If it appears that he has just barely made the initial meld count, has dirtied everything up with wildcards, and has only three or four cards left, then it is probably safe to discard one of the cards he has melded. If he has melded rather easily, most or all of the melds are natural, and he still holds five or more cards, he may be setting you up to discard the card he wants.

• It is fair to ask your opponent how many cards he is holding. If he holds only one card, he cannot pick from the discard pile.

- As your opponent gets close to picking up his Foot or going out, you may find that you need another turn or two to get the cards you need, or to get rid of cards that you do not want. Such situations are when you actually want your opponent to pick from the discard pile—especially if there are a couple of threes—red or black—among the top seven cards. You are buying time and you hope your opponent bites. Of course, unless you know that your opponent holds a specific pair because he picked it from the discard pile earlier, you are only guessing what to throw.

5. **Building a "honey pot."** Some players pick from the discard pile every chance they get. It is as if they cannot help themselves. One way to buy time, that is, a few extra turns before they go out, is to offer them a "honey pot." A honey pot is a discard pile with an irresistible card on top and three or four threes underneath. Unable to resist, the compulsive pile picker must then wait several more turns to deplete the cards he is holding.

Creating a honey pot is not really something you as a player can plan. It is something you take advantage of when the opportunity presents itself, and to make it work you really need to pay attention to the cards your opponent may be holding.

6. **"Priming the pump."** Some Hand & Foot players seem to feel that whatever you discard is also therefore a safe discard for them, figuring that you are just getting rid of the odd orphan card. Sometimes you can play this to your advantage. If you have four or five cards of a certain rank, discard one or two and see if your opponent follows suit. If he does, you can then pick from the discard pile and complete a natural book.

Of course the risks here are:

- Your opponent may not have any cards of that rank to discard to you;

- Your opponent may not be paying as close attention to your discards as you thought; and

- Your opponent may have two such cards and pick the pile himself.

7. **Beware the opponent who has just picked up his Foot,** but does not play any cards from it. He is just looking to pick from the discard pile and the player who discards to him has no idea what to throw.

Picking the Pile

Probably nothing more defines your style of play than how eager or reluctant you are to pick from the discard pile. Some Hand & Foot players, including some of the very best, believe that you should pick from the discard pile at virtually every opportunity. At the same time, there are other, more conservative, but still very good players, who almost never pick from the discard pile. Regardless of where you may sit along that spectrum, the following are things to consider when determining if you want to pick from the discard pile:

1. **Keep track of what has been discarded.** Know what the fourth, fifth, and sixth cards down are. It is okay to grab a few threes, red or black, if it is still early in the round, because you should have time to dispose of them. However, as the round progresses, you may want to first estimate how many turns you will need to get rid of at least the red threes.

   Calculate the tradeoffs if you are trying to decide whether or not to pick from the discard pile. If the second card down completes a natural book, acquiring a red three and a couple of black threes as well might be worth it. However, you must also consider the possible consequences of delaying for two or three turns getting to your Foot or going out. Your opponent will have time to dispose of red threes and complete books. He may also go out, leaving you still holding one of the red threes. Picking from the discard pile simply because you can is not always a good idea.

   Also, if you are playing with a partner, be especially aware of what is in the discard pile:

   • If one partner is ready to go out, the other partner acquiring a couple of red threes by picking from the discard pile may derail his plans.

- If one partner has just picked from the discard pile, and in the process acquires threes and other orphan cards, the other partner may want to avoid also immediately picking from the discard pile. Otherwise they could both be stuck for two or three turns while they try to get rid of them.

2. **Pick the pile, . . . a lot.** The best players of Hand & Foot tend to frequently pick from the discard pile—to some it almost seems an obsession. Their objective is clear—they want as many different cards melded as possible, thus they reduce the likelihood that they will become stalled by an unplayable orphan card. Also, the more cards you have melded the higher your card count and the greater your chance of making books.

The risk here, of course, is the chance of picking up unmatched or otherwise unwanted cards, especially red threes, that you will not be able to get rid of before someone else goes out. Because of this risk, some players are very hesitant to pick from the discard pile before they have picked up their Feet, but feel much freer to go after the discard pile thereafter.

3. **Keep track of your card count.** You need to make the initial meld count before you can pick from the discard pile, and the only card in the discard pile that you can include is the top one. Especially when you get to the 120-point and 150-point initial meld requirements for the third and fourth rounds, respectively, make sure that you have the points that you need. Otherwise you will be laying down and exposing cards to your opponent that you will have to pick up and put back in your Hand because you did not have the minimum initial meld count after all.

4. **Get to your Foot first.** A player who gets to his Foot before every other player has a decided advantage and should more aggressively go after the discard pile. Once the other players have picked up their Feet, he might want to back off a bit.

5. **Wildcards are seldom discarded.** If you need a wildcard, you already know if there is one in the discard pile, and there

likely is not. You will have a better chance of getting one from the stock.

6. **Opponents buying time.** Note if an opponent is trying to feed you desirable cards to get you to pick from the discard pile. What else is in that discard pile? A couple of threes may buy him the time he needs to complete a book.

7. **Pick the pile for discards.** It may seem counterintuitive to deliberately pick from a discard pile full of threes, however, there may be a time in the game when you need a safe discard. A black three freezes out the next player from picking the pile. A red three may discourage the next two or three players from picking the pile, especially if it will cost them a turn in getting to their Feet.

It takes a confident player to pick a pile full of threes, especially more than one red three. To do this, you must be pretty sure that there will be enough turns left in the game to get rid of them.

Picking the Pile Debate: Early and Often versus Caution

There are excellent Hand & Foot players who will advise you to pick from the discard pile at virtually every opportunity. There are also excellent Hand & Foot players who will advise you to be a bit more conservative about picking from the discard pile, especially if you have not yet gotten to your Foot. The pluses and minuses fuel the debate for each side.

Player A subscribes to the more conservative approach. He is reluctant to pick from the discard pile, at least until he has been able to pick up his Foot. Player A is not just concerned about getting stuck with red and black threes. Threes are easy enough to track in the discard pile and he would know what he is getting. His first concern is the other orphan cards and pairs that he would be acquiring as well. Bear in mind, it is very rare to see a wildcard in the discard pile. Wildcards are normally drawn from the stock. Before a player gets to his Foot is when he most needs wildcards. Every orphan card or orphan pair potentially means another turn trying to match it so that it can be melded or discarding it. A lack of wildcards makes this task even more difficult.

Also, picking from the discard pile before Player A has gotten to his Foot means having to lay down the initial meld. He may not want to do that yet. Melding passes information about his status to his opponent. His opponent will have a better idea what to discard and how Player A is progressing toward getting to his Foot. Player A prefers to play his entire Hand all at once and go directly to his Foot. His opponents are usually not prepared when he does that and go into panic mode, depleting the cards that they are holding and sometimes even prematurely dirtying up natural melds.

Player B, meanwhile, believes in the "Pick the Pile Early, Pick the Pile Often" philosophy. Usually, even if the discard pile has threes in it, it is not an issue. Invariably there is time to get rid of them. Acquiring and melding as many different cards as possible is what Player B wants. More different melds means fewer orphans. Picking seven cards from the discard pile means more natural cards to meld, versus two cards from the stock. This translates into more card count, at least, and can translate into more natural books. Thus, even if Player A goes out and catches Player B with a red three, Player B should have more points to offset it.

The extremes in this debate are the player who virtually refuses to pick from a discard pile if it was once touched by a red three, and the player who melds everything just to stop himself from getting carried away excessively picking the pile.

Melding

How a Hand & Foot player melds his cards tends to follow distinctly different strategies when playing as an individual versus when playing with a partner. In general, there are two things to remember about melding:

- When playing as individuals, lay your cards down when you have to, and

- When playing with a partner, lay your cards down when you can.

1. **Playing individually.** You want to give your opponents as little information about your status as possible. Therefore, do not make the beginner's mistake of laying down melds simply because you have the cards or can make the initial meld count. You should not start melding until:

- You want to pick from the discard pile.

- You want to get to your Foot.

- One of your opponents has gotten to his Foot and you fear that he could go out at any time.

- You are holding in your Hand the cards for a natural book and wish to ensure that you get the bonus points.

Be patient, and let your opponents make the mistakes. Remember that whenever you meld your cards, you are also passing along information to your opponent. The less information you pass along, the more you are in control of the game. Once you start laying down cards, your opponent has a better idea what to discard to you and how far along you are toward picking up your Foot or going out.

As a rule of thumb, if it is still early in the game and no one else has really done anything yet, keep your cards in your Hand unless you need to lay them down to pick from the discard pile or to get to your Foot. However, once things start moving with the other players, and especially if an opponent has picked up his Foot, start depleting the cards that you are holding. Throughout the game, hold back your cards as long as you feel it is safe to do so. Make your opponents agonize over what to discard to you.

Also, you do not need to meld everything at once. If you have five jacks, unless you need the card count for the initial meld or want to deplete the cards you are holding, meld only three of them. Hold the other two jacks for a turn or two. You might get lucky and your opponent will discard a jack to you.

2. **Playing with a partner.** Do not wait to meld. Get out there early to help your partner. Your first concern should be for all partners to get to their Feet. If you can, lay down the initial meld for your team as soon as possible. Unlike individual play, in which you want to restrict the information you send out to the other players, you actually want to send information to your partner (and this is the only legal way to do so). Otherwise, he may discard cards that your team can use.

3. **Hold onto your wildcards.** Keep your melds natural as long as you can. Unless you need to use wildcards for the initial meld count, hold onto them. They will come in handy later when you need to get rid of orphan pairs so that you can get to your Foot.

4. **Do not rush to create dirty books.** Natural books are worth 500 bonus points. Dirty books are worth 300 bonus points. Therefore you want as many natural books as possible. Duh. However, if there comes a point in the game when it appears

that your opponent is about to go out, 300 points is better than nothing. If it is all you can do, dirty up your natural melds and get whatever points you can.

5. **Create as many different melds as you can.** In fact, strive to have a meld of each different rank—which means you must pick from the discard pile often! The more different melds you or your team has laid out, the easier it will be for you to play the cards (i.e. get rid of orphan cards and pairs) in your Hand and Foot. It also generates higher card count. However, be mindful of creating natural books. In your rush to create a variety of melds, try to keep as many of them natural as possible. (It is not always possible.)

6. **Hold back pairs from completed books.** Once a book has been completed, if you happen to acquire additional cards of that rank, hold onto them. Do not automatically just add them to the completed book for the card count. A pair of cards from a completed book can still be used to pick from the discard pile. Playing as individuals, they can be added to the completed book to increase card count. Playing with a partner, new melds can be started. It is, however, okay to add cards to a completed book if you need to empty your Hand or go out.

7. **Accumulate the minimum number of books to go out as quickly as you can.** Once you have the minimum, you have the flexibility to make drastic moves, if necessary.

Going Out

Going out feels good. It is the ultimate power play in Hand & Foot and players get a certain feeling of satisfaction from being the one who goes out. However, knowing when to go out, and when not to go out, brings you to the game's bottom line.

Following are things to consider when deciding if it is the right time to go out:

1. **Do not go out prematurely.** Just because a player can go out, does not mean he should. Assess your position in the game. Look at the score at the end of the previous round, then add in the bonus points for books already completed by you and your opponent.

   • If it is one of the early rounds and a couple more turns would allow you a good chance to complete another book or two, hold off going out. Build up points early if you can to offset later shortfalls. When you are ahead of your opponent by a natural book or more, then consider going out, before he has a chance to complete books and accumulate bonus points.

   • If, by your estimate, you are more or less even with your opponent for the point lead, then you probably do not want to go out until something gives you an edge. For instance, count the jokers on either side—if you have three or four more than your opponent you might have the points you need in the card count. If you have the chance, go out before your opponent can play his Foot. Of course, it would help if you can catch your opponent with an undiscarded red three.

- If you are behind by a natural book or more in the last round, there is no point in going out, even if you can. Be patient and continue to play in the hope that you can complete another book or two before your opponent goes out.

2. **Prevent your opponents from building a cushion.** Assess your opponent's position in the game.

- If he is sitting with two or three melds of six natural cards just waiting for the seventh, it is definitely to your advantage to go out, if you can. A natural book that your opponent does not get now is 500 points you do not have to make up later.

- In the earlier rounds, even if you are behind, if you can go out before your opponent can play his Foot, do so. His Foot may well hold a red three or two, and if it does not, you are still preventing him from playing cards that will now count against him. It is also likely that you would prevent him from completing books.

3. **Going out when playing with a partner.** When playing with a partner, you do not have to wait for him to play his Foot to go out. Under normal circumstances, you will need your partner's cards to complete the required number of books to go out. However, there are occasions when one side can go out, even though not all partners' Feet have been played.

- If the score is relatively even, go out if you can catch one or more opponent with his Foot down. Consider it just as likely that an opponent would have a red three in his Hand as would you or your partner—one Foot should more or less cancel out another. Also, you never know how strong your opponent's Foot may be. You might be able to prevent 1,000 to 1,500 bonus points against you.

- If you are behind in the earlier rounds, go out to prevent an opponent from playing his Foot simply to reduce the likely damage. It will mean fewer points to recoup later. In the last round, do not go out unless you have a clear numerical edge.

4. **Count the red threes.** Keep track of any red threes your partner or opponents might have picked up from the discard pile. Bear that information in mind when deciding if you are going out and act appropriately.

Assessing Hands

When you first look at your Hand, right away you should have a pretty good idea how many turns it will take to make the initial meld or get to your Foot. When you first look at your Foot, right away you should have a pretty good idea how many turns it will take to go out.

This is actually important information to have. Knowing your status in the round and in the game should greatly affect how you play, especially if you estimate that the number of turns you need to do what you want to do differs substantially from the number of turns you estimate your opponent needs to do what he wants to do.

Assess your hand. The status of the cards you hold changes with each turn.

- First count the threes. Regardless of whether you decide to draw from the stock or pick from the discard pile, each three, red or black, will have to be discarded in a separate turn.

- Next look at the orphan cards and the orphan pairs. Estimate the minimum number of turns it will take to either meld or discard each if you only draw two cards at a time from the stock.

- Consider the discard pile and if picking the top seven cards will help or exacerbate your situation. If picking from the discard pile would help, are you holding any pairs that your opponent is likely to throw to you?

Assess your opponent's hand. After you have assessed your own cards and have determined the number of turns you need to do what you want to do, match that against what you are able to ascertain about the cards your opponent holds. What you are holding is only half the equation. What your opponent holds is just as important in determining how many turns you have left in the round. Complicating this is the fact that if your opponent is any kind of Hand & Foot player at all, he is trying to keep that information from you.

- Count the threes. If your opponent has picked from the discard pile, and what he has picked includes any threes, red or black, you know that you have at least that many turns before he can get to his Foot or go out, as the case may be. He may have more threes or other orphans, as well, but of this you cannot be certain.

- Does he have the minimum number of completed books in order to go out? If he does, you have a problem. You are lucky to have a turn to play or dispose of whatever you can from among the cards that you hold—and you should do so. That is unless it is the fourth round and to do so would ruin any chance that you may have of catching up.

- What is the score? If your opponent is behind by a couple of books, he is likely going to hang in until he can complete them. Look at his melds. How many cards does he need to complete the books that he needs to take the lead?

Tricks & Strategies

Beyond simply knowing the rules of the game, following are some of the tried and tested strategies and a few tricks for playing and, more often than not, winning at Hand & Foot.

The object of the game is to win, of course, by scoring more points than your opponent(s). Just how you go about doing this can determine if you come in first, last, or somewhere in between when the final score is tallied.

Someone who plays Hand & Foot should expect to lay down a variety of melds and steadily build on them until he is able to deplete his Hand and pick up his Foot. He will then play the cards in his Foot until he has the minimum of one natural book and one dirty book, allowing him to go out. Simple enough—however, everyone else in the game is trying to do the same thing, and thus it becomes a race. Sometimes, a player really does not have much choice, because the cards he gets pretty much dictate what he can do. Usually, though, how the cards are played can improve a player's standing at the end of the game.

Following are a few tips that can form the basis of a winning strategy for a novice to average Hand & Foot player:

1. **Get to your Foot!** There is no one thing that a Hand & Foot player can do to help himself more in any round of Hand & Foot, whether playing as an individual or with a partner, than playing out his Hand and getting to his Foot as quickly as possible. This has to be his primary short-term goal throughout the game.

    •   The Foot is the unknown. It holds cards that you expect will help you. However, more importantly, it may hold cards that can hurt you—red threes. A couple of red threes in your Foot can wipe out a thousand-point lead. You have to get rid of them!

- This philosophy holds especially true when playing with a partner. Not only do you want to get to your own Foot as quickly as possible, you want to do anything that you can to help your partner get to his Foot. This generally means starting as many different melds as possible.

- Get to your Foot as quickly as possible, even if it means dirtying up every natural meld that you have to clear out your Hand. The chance to get to your Foot is not always there. On the next turn, you could easily draw two orphans (or two threes), and then you are stuck. Once you have gotten to your Foot and have disposed of any red threes that it may contain, you are in control and free to maneuver and start new natural melds.

2. **Hold back a wildcard.** If you can, that is. Unless you have reached a point in the round where you must play or dispose of whatever cards that you can, holding back a wildcard gives you a great deal of flexibility in play. It allows you to meld an orphaned pair. It allows you to score a quick 300 points on a dirty book if the time is right to make such a move. In almost any situation, having a wildcard can come in really handy.

3. **Hold back pairs that could be melded.** Novice players tend to add cards to a meld as soon as they get them. However, more experienced players will hold pairs of melded cards back. In trying to decide what to discard, opponents are inclined to throw to you something that you have melded, in the belief that such cards are safer because you likely would not still be holding two of them. With some players, that line of reasoning just does not work. There are some truly devious players who will have six cards melded toward a book, yet still hold back a pair intent on picking from the discard pile.

It can be tricky business if you hold these extra cards too long. Meld them down and clear them out of your hand when you sense someone else could go out at any time.

4. **Pay attention to what everyone else is doing, . . . but keep it to yourself.** Every now and then you run into a player who can be very subtle, and get to his Foot almost surreptitiously without anyone else noticing. Always watch what the other player does during his turns. If you notice him doing something—like very quietly picking up his Foot or completing books while someone else is talking—take note of it as it concerns your own game, but do not say anything. Everyone else is your opponent, as well, and you do not want to help them.

5. **Play a psychological game.** If you are playing against a really good opponent who does not do as well when distracted, then keep talking to them. Better yet, keep them laughing. Watch for opponent cues—or as they are called in poker, "tells"—that indicate what they might do next. For instance, some players really start to fidget when they are about to go out. Also, watch yourself for any cues you may inadvertently be giving.

6. **Watch the other players and be aware of your relative status in the round and the game.** It is time to start getting nervous when the first opponent gets to his Foot. Get even more nervous when the first opponent has the minimum number of books to go out. Depending on your own situation, it might be wise to deplete the cards that you are holding as best you can and make whatever points you can.

7. **Go out to prevent your opponents from playing their Feet.** When playing with partners, it can happen that your team is able to go out, but that it might otherwise be disadvantageous to do so. Perhaps you are well behind in the scoring. However, if you or your partner can go out before one or more of the partners of the opposing team can play their Feet, the second team will likely be prevented from scoring significant points.

They may even be caught with a red three or two that can set them back in scoring.

If you are playing as partners and find yourself in the position of being able to go out before your partner has played his Foot, evaluate the situation. Would the likely benefit to your team outweigh the likely cost? You can assume that one Foot is more or less equal to the next and that a red three is just as likely to appear in your opponent's Foot as in your partner's Foot.

Consider a scenario of two teams of two partners each. Your team has the minimum number of books required to go out, but your partner has not yet played his Foot. One player on the other team has already played his Foot, while his partner has just picked up his, but will not be able to play it until the next turn. If you are able to go out in your next turn, you probably should do so, before the second player on the other team can play his Foot. By going out, you will prevent your opponent from playing the cards in his Foot and potentially completing one or more books for bonus points.

Remember, when a second partner on a team is given the chance to play his Foot, frequently that team will be able to go out. Any time you can deny an opponent his Foot on equal or better terms, it is probably to your advantage to do so, either by catching him with red threes to set him back, or at least by denying him the points he would have had, had he played it.

Caution! This is aggressive play and you can set yourself back just as easily as you can set your opponent back. If you have a healthy lead, you should probably not risk it. If the game is close, it is a judgement call. If you are behind, you have nothing to lose.

8. **The "fake going out query."** This one borders on unethical. Playing with a partner, suppose you have reached a point where one team has the minimum number of dirty books they need to go out and is only one or two cards away from getting the natural

books they need, as well. A partner on the other team asks if they can go out. The other partner says, "No." The first partner therefore does not go out, but simply takes a regular turn. Because of the query, the other team, fearing that they could be caught with unplayed cards and incomplete books for no bonus points decides to "dirty up" their remaining natural melds with wildcards to at least get the 300 points for a dirty book. They are thus stuck for a number of turns to come, unable to go out for the lack of the minimum number of natural books, and no natural melds to build on. The faking team, on the other hand, has bought time to complete the books they need to build enough bonus count to win.

The stars really have to be in alignment to make this one work. It needs to be a close game, the other team has to fall for the ruse, and the cards must cooperate. However, if you can pull it off, the other team will be squawking about it all the way home.

Hand & Foot Etiquette

Like any card game, Hand & Foot follows certain rules of etiquette, which can make it a more enjoyable game for everyone.

1. **Discarding ends a player's turn.** Plain and simple, when a player throws his discard, he is done for that turn. There should be no further melding of cards after that until the player's next turn.

   A player who has just picked from the discard pile should not try to do the rest of the players a favor by not holding up the game. That is, he should not discard so that the next player can take his turn, all the while continuing to sort through and meld the cards he has just acquired. Each player completes the actions of his turn before he discards or he waits until his next turn.

2. **No changing your mind on a discard.** A player should not discard one card, then change his mind because he thinks has made a mistake. Once a player has let go of a card, it becomes the official discard and that player's turn is over.

3. **No backtracking on picking the pile.** A player should not change his mind about picking from the discard pile just because he realizes that under the top card he wanted are three or four threes he did not want. Once a player has started to take cards from the discard pile, he is committed to it.

   Also, it is not ethical to check what cards are under the top card of the discard pile before deciding to pick from it. A player should be paying attention and keeping track of what has been discarded.

4. **Count out the cards when picking from the discard pile.** The other players have a right to verify that you are taking exactly seven cards from the top when picking the pile. Those cards should be exposed (face up) and counted out in plain view, where everyone can see them.

5. **Lay out the initial meld before picking from the discard pile.** The other players are entitled to verify that you have the minimum initial meld requirement before you take any cards from the discard pile. Remember, only the top card can be used in the initial meld count.

6. **There is no order of play within a turn.** A player's turn begins when he either draws from the stock or picks from the discard pile. It ends when he discards. Anything he does between those actions does not become final until he does discard. That means he is free to change his mind about how he melds and can reverse any play that he has made.

Also, all plays within a turn are considered simultaneous. This means, for instance, that if a player has melded six jacks, he cannot within the same turn play first a wildcard, then another jack on that meld and call it a dirty book. If he wishes it to be a dirty book (in order to go out) he would have to wait until the next turn to add the other jack to the book as additional count.

7. **Etiquette With Partners.** Essentially, the only etiquette unique to Hand & Foot play with partners that is not an issue with individual players is "**table talk**." That is, one partner letting another partner know what cards he has so as to affect the way the partner plays his cards.

An example of this would be if one player either told or signaled in some way to his partner that he has a pair of kings, so that the partner would not discard any kings he might have. It is okay for a player to announce what he has melded. That is supposed to be knowledge for everyone in the game. However, one partner may not play "Go Fish." That is, for instance, ask if their team has queens melded, which in fact they do not, because it would be a signal that he has a queen.

Also, if one player is passing cards to his partner to be melded, he must also give the instructions on where they are to be played, without consulting his partner. The player who is melding the cards for his team should not decide how his partner's wildcards are to be played.

Laying down the initial meld also presents a problem. If one player starts to lay down cards for the fourth round initial meld of 150 points, where everyone can see them, then supposedly makes a mistake in adding them up, his partner has seen a substantial number of cards he is holding. In one rule variation, there is even a 500-point penalty for miscounting the cards in the initial meld in a game with partners.

8. **Correcting Mistakes.** Occasionally someone inadvertently draws three cards from the stock instead of two or plays someone else's Foot. As a general rule, mistakes should be corrected as simply as possible. Additional cards drawn, whether someone has seen what they are or not, should be returned to their previous place on top of the stock. If someone picks up and plays someone else's Foot by mistake, that person's Foot should be given as the other person's replacement (one Foot is supposed to be treated the same as another).

Hosting a Tournament

Hand & Foot makes a terrific social activity. It is both fun and challenging for anyone old enough to understand the concept of card games in general. Once people have learned to play Hand & Foot and have taught it to virtually all of their friends, there comes a point when they want to know who is the best. If you just have to know, then it is time to get everyone together for a Hand & Foot tournament.

Organizing a Hand & Foot tournament is a lot of work. Playing in a Hand & Foot tournament is a lot of fun. Following are some of the things that have been done in previous tournaments that have made them work.

1. **How big?** The first step in organizing a Hand & Foot tournament is deciding how big you want it to be. The actual number of players who will be participating determines how they will be seated. Probably the minimum number of players you can have and still call it a tournament is sixteen, who would be seated at four tables of four players each.

   Four or more tables for sixteen or more players also means coming up with considerable space to hold them. Give due consideration to an appropriate venue.

2. **How long?** From our experience, everyone playing four games seems appropriate for a tournament. If you play fewer than four games, it seems as if luck becomes too big a factor. More than four games can make for a long day. In fact, four games of four rounds each can take a long time, which is why for tournaments, games are sometimes shortened to three rounds, skipping the 60-point initial meld round and starting with the 90-point initial meld requirement, then moving up to the 120-point round and the 150-point round.

3. Redistributing winners. There are really two ways to do this.

A. Using the 16-player, 4-table example, number the tables 1, 2, 3 & 4. Randomly assign players to seats at each table for the first game. After the first game, the first and second place finishers at Table #4 move up to Table #3 to play the third and fourth place finishers at that table. The first and second place finishers from Table #3 move up to Table #2 to play the third and fourth place finishers at that table, and so on. The first and second place finishers at Table #1, however stay there and the third and fourth place finishers move to Table #4. This process is repeated after each game of the tournament.

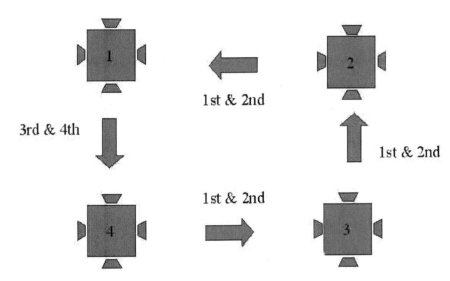

Therefore, if you have been at Table #1 all day, it means that you have been winning all day. And if you have been at Table #4 all day, it means that you have been losing all day.

This method can be adjusted for odd numbers of players. With 17 players, seat five at Table #1 and four at the rest. With 18 players, seat five at Tables #1 and #2, and four at the rest, and so on.

B. Again using the 16-player, 4-table example, number the tables 1, 2, 3 & 4. Again randomly assign players to seats at each table for the first game. However, after the first game all the players who came in first at their respective tables move to Table #1, all the second place finishers move to Table #2, and so on. This process is repeated after each game of the tournament.

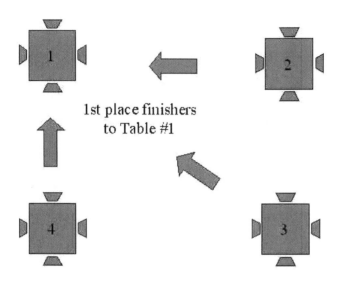

1st place finishers
to Table #1

Again, staying at Table #1 means you have been winning, and staying at Table #4 means that you have been losing.

This method only works with 16, 25, or 36 players—who can be equally distributed—in the tournament, or tournament segments*, seated at tables of four, five, and six players, respectively.

4. **Tournament scoring.** (Continuing with four players at a table) Tournament leaders are determined by the number of players defeated in each game. After the first game, a player who comes in first at his table, and in the process defeats three opponents, scores three points. The player who comes in second at the

---

* Large tournaments may require that players be divided into segments consisting of 16, 25, or 36 players each.

same table and has defeated only two opponents scores two points. The player who comes in third scores one point, and the player who comes in fourth scores zero.

- After two games, a player who wins the first game but comes in second in the second game has a total of five points for defeating five opponents, and so on throughout the tournament.

- At the end of four games, if one player has won every game, he scores a perfect 12 points.

5. **Score sheets.** Score sheets for each table should be collected after each game. Someone should be keeping an overall tally of the tournament players and verify their scores. It is also interesting to keep track of tournament statistics, such as who made a perfect cut the most number of times, who had the highest point score for the tournament, who scored the fewest points for a game, etc.

6. **Playoff game and championship game.** After the four games of the tournament are played, the four players with the best won-loss records play in a championship round. One hand is played, with a minimum initial meld requirement of 150 points. Whoever wins the championship round, wins the tournament.

If one or more players tie for the fourth seat at the championship table, there is a playoff round. One hand is played, with a minimum initial meld requirement of 120 points. Whoever wins the playoff round, moves on to the championship round.

7. **Prizes.** Besides just bragging rights, the winner should get something—a certificate, a medal, a trophy—that he can take home with him. You may also want to recognize the person who came in last place, if for no other reason than for being a good sport. Consider, as well, recognizing the statistical distinctions—highest point total for the tournament, for a game, and for a round; most perfect cuts for the tournament; etc.

8. **Charity tournament.** If there are enough Hand & Foot players in a community, hosting a tournament could be a good way to raise money for a worthy cause. For instance, if a youth organization, such as the Boy Scouts, is looking for a way to raise funds, rather than a car wash or selling candy door to door, they could host a Hand & Foot tournament at $5 per participant. They could make additional money by selling refreshments. The hosting organization would provide the venue and serve as the tournament officials. Winners all the way around.

Memorable Hand & Foot Personalities

Alice (The Shark)

This flamboyant player loves to dominate the conversation and control the game. There is no one better at assessing a hand and her own status at any point in the game. She will even assess her position at the table and try to arrange seating so that she can discard to whom she wishes, and receive discards from whom she wishes.

By nature, Alice is extroverted and outgoing. In a tournament, she will wear something playing card-themed that everyone will notice and comment on, and her table will be the most boisterous. Half of this is just Alice being Alice, but half of it is Alice distracting her opponents from concentrating on their games. You see, while everyone else is looking at her funny hat or trying to follow the good gossip she is dishing, Alice sees and mentally notes everything that is going on in the game. She knows what cards are in the discard pile—not just the top seven, but at least the next seven as well. If there is a card that she wants, she will continue to pick from the pile in successive turns until she gets it. If you have picked from the discard pile, she knows which cards you have played, which you have discarded, and which you still hold. She also knows, probably within twenty or thirty points, what her score and what your score would be if someone were to go out.

Based on all the information Alice has processed, she knows when to play aggressively and when to be patient. Her opponents usually watch helplessly while she racks up big points by completing book after book in the early rounds so that everyone else is left desperately playing catch-up for the rest of the game. If necessary, however, Alice will play her own masterful game of catch-up and keep the last round going as long as it takes for her to accumulate the points she needs to win. Alice has even been known to play her initial meld and the rest of her Hand (without discarding), go directly to her Foot, play it, and go out, all in the same turn. Her playing style can best be described as a tightening vise. Once she has you where she wants you, she just keeps applying the pressure.

Weakness: Control. Alice has to have it. If she is not running the conversation, she is herself distracted by it. When she gets significantly behind in points, she becomes quiet and intense. Alice's own strategy for winning is what works best against her. But the pressure has to be unrelenting, because Alice will take advantage of any opening offered. Good luck beating her!

Mandy (The Cat)

According to her children, this sweet little grandmother is the consummate competitor who has never *let* anyone win at any game—cards, dominoes, checkers—even if her opponent is just four or five years old. Everyone has to *earn* his or her victory. Mandy is a seasoned Canasta master who likes to set traps. After you have been caught for the umpteenth time you start to feel like a mouse that is just being softened up.

The key to Mandy's strategy and her success is picking from the discard pile any and every time she can . . . and she seems able to pick from the pile every turn, no matter what you discard to her. She manages to do this by holding back pairs—pairs of cards that she has not yet melded and pairs of cards that she has melded. She even holds back pairs of cards that could be played on a meld of five or six to complete a book. She has been known to hold six cards of the same rank in her hand to entice it as a discard—sometimes even discarding one or two of them to prime the pump.

Needless to say, Mandy is after a variety of cards. She wants to have a meld of everything, and frequently she does. She lines up her melds in order, from lowest to highest, so that she can quickly identify what is missing. With melds of everything, she virtually always has a play to make. Also, because of the variety and quantity of cards Mandy acquires, she always seems to be just one card away from going out. One of her more memorable plays was having six cards on two different natural melds, then in her next turn drawing one of each to complete two natural books, and go out.

One of Mandy's favorite ploys is, in the later rounds where 120 or 150 is needed for the initial meld, holding back pairs of the five-count cards—fours, fives, sixes, and sevens. Since an orphan five-count is of little use in building a big initial meld, it is frequently the discard of choice of her opponents. She thus has the opportunity to capture it and the next six cards.

Weakness: You would think that a person so fond of setting traps would recognize the one that she herself cannot resist. Mandy is a compulsive pile picker. Even when she knows there are a couple of red threes just below, she cannot help but pick from the discard pile. Therefore, the honey pot almost always gets her. The problem is, she usually gets you first. And even if she gets caught holding a red three, with all the cards she has acquired, she usually has built up enough bonus points to compensate.

Alan (The Engineer)

We all knew Alan was a bright guy, but maybe, we thought, he just was not particularly competitive. We taught him the basics of Hand & Foot and he seemed to grasp them well enough, but it did not seem like he was getting into the spirit of play. For the next year or so, whenever a group of us got together to play the game, Alan just seemed to go through the motions—not picking from the discard pile very often, never going out, always finishing third or fourth in a five-person or six-person game.

Then came the first Hand & Foot tournament. Out of 17 players, including the previously mentioned Alice and Mandy, who do you think won? Alan, of course. And he has been a consistent winner ever since.

What happened? We had forgotten that Alan is, by profession, an engineer. For that year before the first tournament, Alan did what engineers do, gather data and test tolerances. When it came time to play for keeps, he was ready. Statistically, at least, he knew how long he could hold onto his cards before melding, how many turns would remain to get rid of the red threes contained therein if he picked from the discard pile, and how long it would take to get the points he needed to win. He could also sense approximately how many of a particular card were left in the stock (and thus which meld to dirty up) and what would be a safe discard based on how many cards of that rank were still unaccounted for. Alan had become a logical machine.

Weakness: Playing a straight forward game of Hand & Foot, Alan is going to win almost every time. However, being a logical machine, the unexpected and unconventional jams his gears. The way to beat him is to take advantage of the atypical situations the cards may allow—do not meld until you have to (withhold information), get to your foot quickly, go out early. Play aggressively—hold onto black threes for when you need them, and discard wildcards or cards that you have melded, if necessary, to disrupt the natural flow of the game. Nevertheless, expect that the statistics will always work to Alan's advantage.

Sandy and Susan (The Opportunists)

Not quite the Venus and Serena Williams of Hand & Foot, sisters Sandy and Susan are nonetheless indistinguishable in their deliberate and opportunistic play. They are actually stealth players who manage to stay just below everyone else's radar. They each play a very quiet game, usually unnoticed just behind the leader in points, that is, until the leader makes a mistake.

I sometimes wonder what they must have been like growing up—competitively driven siblings silently playing an intense game of Monopoly, watching each other's every move with icy, unblinking stares. What makes the play of Sandy and Susan so unnerving is the stuff you never see coming. There always seems to come a point in a game against one of them when someone else says, "You're out? I didn't even know you picked up your Foot!" The sisters are not easily distracted. They watch the cards, all the cards. In addition to the cards that you have melded and discarded, they know how many cards you have left in your hand, and probably how you have arranged them. It is as if each has a mental checklist of things to note before making their plays.

The key to the sisters' strategy is patience and waiting for the breaks, whether in the form of a few lucky cards or someone else's mistake. They themselves do not make mistakes and their solid style of play is probably the least dependent on luck.

Weakness: Though calling them overly cautious might not be exactly accurate, Sandy and Susan are certainly risk averse. They let the other players take the risks and make every attempt to capitalize if things go bad. However, at the same time the sisters do not reap the rewards of calculated risks that go well for the risk-taker. So the way to beat either Sandy or Susan is to make no mistakes and get lucky. Yeah, right!

Memorable Hand & Foot Moments

A Strategy Discovered

Bert, Ernie, Lucy, and Ethel were playing as two teams of two, the men against the women. The score was about even going into the fourth round and the fourth round itself was running neck and neck. Bert and Lucy were each able to pick up and play their respective Feet, while Ernie and Ethel were not.

Then, in his turn, Bert, who had played his Foot, completed the last of the requisite number of books (two naturals and three dirties) and went out. Aghast, his partner Ernie said, "What the hell are you doing? I haven't gotten to my Foot yet!"

Bert was himself shocked by his mistake. "Oh no! I thought you played it!"

"No, I haven't!"

The subsequent point tally showed that Ernie's unplayed Foot contained about 120 points, but no red threes. The same could not be said for Ethel's unplayed Foot. It contained two red threes. The men won the game by over 1,000 points.

After the final score was announced, Bert, who had not been paying attention to his partner's status and had prematurely gone out without consulting his partner, decided, "You know, this could be a strategy."

Despite his blundering into it, Bert was right. There is nothing in the rules that says all partners have to play their Feet before their side can go out. As long the side has the minimum number of completed books and as long as one partner can play all his cards, they can go out any time they wish. Sometimes it is aggressive play, sometimes it is a last ditch effort. Whatever the motivation, taking a chance by denying your opponents the opportunity to play all of their cards can pay off.

Bone-Headed Finishes by Bone-Headed Partners

Number One: Stan, Oliver, Patty, and Maxine were playing as two teams of two players each, and as usual, it was the men against the women. This was an extremely close game, with each player on both sides hoping to draw the one card that would allow them to go out. Finally, holding just one card, Stan drew two cards from the stock. One of them was the card needed to complete the last book for his side.

"Would you like to go out?" he asked Oliver.

"It is going to be close, but yes, let's do it," was Oliver's response.

Stan had two other cards to play—a six and a deuce. He put the six on a meld of three other sixes and discarded the deuce, rather than play the deuce on a meld of six cards (which would have yielded a dirty book and 300 bonus points) and discard the six. The scores were tallied and the men lost the game by less than 100 points.

Number Two: It was a big game—nine players on three teams of three. One team consisted of three brothers, Huey, Dewey, and Louie. The brothers were ahead after three rounds, but the fourth round was not going so well. Huey had been able to pick up and play his Foot. Dewey and Louie kept drawing orphan cards that prevented them from depleting their Hands.

Late in the round, after several frustrating turns of not being able to do anything to help his team's prospects, Dewey watched as Huey drew two cards and discarded one without laying anything down. "Nothing new to meld?" asked Dewey.

Drawing attention to the fact that all of their melds included wildcards, Huey said in a tone as if to state the obvious, "We need naturals!"

At which point Louie, in the same tone, but louder said, "But we need to get to our Feet!"

It was too late for Huey to correct the situation. One of the other sides went out before he could play again. The brothers lost, big time, because a couple of red threes were contained in Dewey's and Louie's unplayed Feet. As it turned out, Huey held pairs and wildcards that if melded could have allowed Dewey and Louie to play out their Hands.

Number Three: It was late in the fourth round, Willie and Lester against Thelma and Louise, with the women ahead as usual. With the right draw, the women could go out and leave the men in their dust. Instead, Thelma decided to pick from the discard pile.

The top card on the pile did not even yield a book, but if she had been paying attention, Thelma would have known that there were four red threes among the next six cards below it. She was able to discard one.

On the very next play, Willie went out. The 1,500 negative points Thelma still held were enough to drop her team's score below the men's score. Good pick!

Top Ten Things That Will Make Opponent Sputter

10. Going from your Hand straight to your Foot without discarding and thus not having to wait until your next turn.

9. Going out before he has played his Foot.

8. Going out after he has picked from a discard pile containing more than one red three.

7. Winning by less than 100 points after a perfect cut.

6. Coming from behind to win after catching your opponent with a red three.

5. Picking from the discard pile using the only two cards you are holding.

4. Drawing two cards that each complete a natural book.

3. Picking from the discard pile after "priming the pump."

2. Going out before he has melded any cards.

1. Picking up your Foot, playing all the cards contained in it, and going out, all in the same turn.

Variations and Alternate Rules for Hand & Foot

Hand & Foot itself appears to be a regional variation of Canasta. My wife and I learned it from someone, who learned it from someone else, who learned it from someone in Florida. We have encountered people who have learned it or have seen it played various other places both in the United States and overseas.

My research, which includes sites on the Internet, indicates that the rules of Hand & Foot seem to vary depending on where and from whom you learn the game. The rest of this book has covered what I consider to be the standard rules. Following in this chapter are some of the more common "regional" variations and alternate rules to the game of Hand & Foot.

The "Whiners' Round"

There are occasions when a person or team playing Hand & Foot seems to pull it out of a hat and win by shear luck, or so their opponents would have you believe. Many is the time that people who have failed to prevail in a spirited game of Hand & Foot have contended that if they had played just one more round, they would have won. To accommodate, there is what is known as the "**Whiners' Round**". A whiners' round is a fifth round of Hand & Foot, after the standard four, that some believe can settle a dispute over who really is the better player. A whiners' round is played like any other round, except the minimum initial meld requirement is 180 points.

If, after five rounds, there is still something to be settled, a sixth round, called a **"Double Whiners' Round,"** can be played with an initial meld requirement of 210 points.

Book variations

Different bonus values: Instead of 500 points for a natural book and 300 points for a dirty book, the values are decreased to 300 points and 100 points, respectively.

Book of wildcards: Wildcards are allowed to be melded separately. A complete book consisting entirely of wildcards is worth 1,500 bonus points.

Book of red threes: A player or partnership has the option to create a book of red threes, however there is a catch. Only natural books may be created (no wildcards), and all threes must be held in the hand until there are seven and comprise a complete book. A book of red threes is worth 3,500 bonus points. The threes have no individual positive card count value, but do still count a negative 500 points against the player holding them if not part of a complete book.

> **Note:** If only two people are playing, using three decks of cards, there are only six red threes to be played. There must be at least three players and four decks of cards in the game to make this rule work.

Multiple books of the same rank

This variation allows an individual player to start new melds of a specific rank after a book has been completed. That is, if a player already has a book of jacks, he is allowed to start another meld of jacks, rather than just add card count to the existing book.

Increasing value of perfect cuts

Instead of the flat 100 points awarded for each perfect cut at the start of each round, the first time in a game that a player cuts exactly 22 cards, the player is awarded 100 bonus points. The second time in the same game that a player cuts exactly 22 cards is worth 200 bonus points, the third time 300 points, and the fourth time, 400 points.

Variations on picking from the discard pile:

Five instead of seven: When a player picks from the discard pile, instead of the top seven cards, he is allowed/required to take the top five cards.

Entire pile: When a player picks from the discard pile, rather than the top seven cards, he is allowed/required to take all the cards in the discard pile.

Down to a red three: According to this variation, whenever a red three is discarded, all the previous discards below it are from that point on in the round removed from play. If someone picks from the discard pile thereafter, instead of the top seven cards of the pile, he collects however many cards have been discarded down to the most recently discarded red three. (The number of cards can be more or fewer than seven.)

Going out variations

Double books for fourth round: This variation requires that instead of one natural book and one dirty book for each round, for the fourth round only, a minimum of two natural books and two dirty books are required for a player to go out.

Book of wildcards required: In order to go out in each round, a player must have completed a natural book, a dirty book, and a book of wildcards.

Replenishing the Stock

When the stock is depleted and there no cards remain to draw, left in order the top seven cards are removed from the discard pile and become the top of the new discard pile. The remaining cards in the discard pile are turned over and become the new stock. These cards are also left in order—not shuffled! Play continues as normally.

In games where the stock is depleted and replenished several times, the stock can come to contain nothing but threes. In such cases, the round can be ended by mutual agreement among the players and the cards held in the players' hands do not count against them.

Playing through to the Foot on a short count

It doesn't happen very often, but when a player is able to deplete his or her Hand, but does not have the minimum card count for an initial meld, the player is allowed to continue on to his or her Foot, expecting that the Foot will provide the remaining count required. If the player tries, but it turns out that the Foot does not provide the necessary count to meet the initial meld minimum, the Foot is put back down, the Hand is picked back up, and the player is penalized 500 points.

Playing for Money

Hand & Foot is not normally played for money, but it is a competition and someone is bound to want to place a bet on the outcome. One way to do this is for a penny a point. If two people are playing against each other, the loser owes the winner a penny for each point difference in their scores. For example, if one player has a final score of 6,620 points and the other has a final score of 5,480, the difference between them is 1,140 points. The player with the lower score owes his opponent $11.40.

If there is more than one player, you can still play for pennies, or whatever amount you choose, but calculating the payoff is a bit more complicated. First you must tally the sum of all the final scores. For example, if four people are playing and their final scores are 7,120 points, 6,130 points, 5,820 points, and 3,330 points, add the scores all together for a total of 22,400 points. Divide that total by the number of players, in this case four, for a total of 5,600. Each player then owes the game pot $56.00. From the pot of $224.00, each player claims the amount that corresponds to his score, respectively $71.20, $61.30, $58.20, and $33.30. Thus, the player who came in first, with 7,120 points, wins $15.20 ($71.20 minus

---

$56.00). The player who came in second, with 6,130 points, wins $5.30. The player who came in third, with 5,820 points, wins $2.20, and the player who came in fourth place, with 3,330 points, lost a total of $22.70.

As you can see, with the scores possible in Hand & Foot, even playing for pennies can get into worthwhile money. (Every red three is worth $5.)

Glossary

Book: A completed **book** is a melded set of at least seven cards of the same rank. A **natural book** consists entirely of natural cards—no wildcards—and has a bonus value of 500 points. A mixed or **dirty book** includes at least one wildcard and has a bonus value of 300 points.

Card count: The total combined value of cards used to comprise an initial meld or the point tally at the end of a round.

Card value: The following values are assigned to each respective card in a game of Hand & Foot:

Joker	50 points
Aces & Deuces	20 points
8, 9, 10, J, Q, K	10 points
4, 5, 6, 7	5 points
Black 3	-5 points*
Red 3	-500 points*

Depleted stock: If no player has yet gone out when the cards in the stock are depleted, play for that round ends unless the next player is able and wishes to draw from the discard pile. Play would thus continue until a successive player in his turn either cannot or does not wish to draw from the discard pile. If play for a round concludes due to a depleted stock, the cards that remain in all players Hands and Feet count against their respective point totals.

Dirty up: A natural meld is "dirtied up" when a wildcard is added to it.

---

*   If held in the Hand or Foot when someone else goes out.

Discard pile: The pile of exposed discards to which each player must add another card at the conclusion of each turn. A players may opt to pick the top seven cards from the discard pile rather than draw two from the stock at the at the start of his turn if he can match the top card with two natural cards of the same rank from among the cards that he is holding, and if he has met the initial meld requirement for that round.

Foot: This is a player's second hand. After the Hand has been played, a player may pick up and play the cards contained in his Foot. If a player has the required number of books, when all the cards contained in his Foot are played, that player may go out.

Going out: A player may go out when he has completed the required number of books and gets rid of the last card in his Foot, ending play for that round.

Going out query: When playing with one or more partner, a player who is able to go out is allowed to ask his partner(s) only one question—"May I go out?" The partner(s) in turn may respond only either "yes" or "no." No other discussion pertaining to the game is allowed and no other information may be exchanged between or among partners. The player doing the asking is not bound by the response(s) of his partner(s).

Hand: The first half of the "Hand & Foot" combination. The Hand initially consists of 11 cards, but increases as additional cards are drawn. All of the cards contained in the Hand must be played—either melded or discarded—before a player may pick up his Foot.

Honey pot: When the top card of the discard pile is very desirable and tempting for the next player to pick, but the next six cards include mostly threes, the pile is called a "honey pot." A honey pot is a trap used by one player or team to delay the opposing side's going out (because it takes one turn each to dispose of threes). Luring an opponent into picking a honey pot is generally considered a desperation move when one side is close to going out, but the other side needs another turn or two to completely play out cards or accumulate the points needed to win.

Initial meld requirement: The first meld by each side in a round must meet the minimum initial meld requirement set for that round. That is, the point value of the cards melded in the initial meld must total no less than the initial meld requirement set for each respective round. The initial meld requirements for each round are:

1st Round	60 points
2nd Round	90 points
3rd Round	120 points
4th Round	150 points

Meld: A meld consists of three to six cards of the same rank, laid out and exposed for all players in the game to see. A meld may include wildcards to substitute for natural cards, but natural cards must at all times outnumber wildcards. When a seventh card is added to a meld, it becomes a completed book.

Orphan Card: An unmatched card that, by itself cannot be melded.

Orphan Pair: A pair of cards that lack a third card, either natural or wildcard, that would allow it to be melded.

Perfect cut: At the start of a round of Hand & Foot, each player attempts to cut exactly 22 cards off the top of the stock. These cards are then divided into two piles of 11 cards each, one pile to be that player's Hand, the other pile to be the Foot of the next player, moving clockwise around the table. Thus at the beginning of each round, before actual play begins, each player has an 11-card Hand and an 11-card Foot. If a player has cut less than 22 cards, additional cards as needed are drawn from the stock. If a player has cut more than 22 cards, the excess cards are returned to the stock. If a player has cut exactly 22 cards, a **perfect cut**, that player is awarded 100 bonus points.

Picking the pile: Each player begins his respective turn by either drawing two cards from the stock or picking from the discard pile. To pick from the discard pile, a player must meet two criteria. He must have among the cards he is holding (not melded or contained in an unrevealed Foot) two natural cards of the same rank as the top card on the pile (a natural card and a wildcard are not acceptable), and he must have met the initial meld requirement for that round (the top card is the only card from the pile that can be included in the initial meld). If a player can meet those criteria, he must take the top seven cards from the discard pile (the top card he has matched and the next six) if there are at least that many cards in the pile. If there are not at least seven cards in the discard pile, he must take the entire pile. If there are at least seven cards in the discard pile, a player who picks the pile may not choose to take less than seven cards. Threes and wildcards freeze the discard pile and may not be picked, regardless of what cards the next player holds.

Priming the pump: A player may hold three or more cards of the same rank and discard one of them in the hope of leading his opponent to mistakenly believe that it is a safe discard for himself and subsequently also discard a card of that same rank. When this happens, the first player has in effect "primed the pump" and will be able to pick from the discard pile in his next turn.

Stock: The unexposed combined multiple deck of cards from which players draw two cards to begin their respective turns if they cannot or do not wish to pick from the discard pile.

Table talk: When playing with partners, giving information that may assist a partner in playing his cards—such as which cards to hold or discard, or where to meld a wildcard—is considered "table talk." Table talk is not permitted at any point during a partnership game of Hand & Foot.

Whiner's round and double whiner's round: When a player or team of partners playing Hand & Foot manages to pull out a victory by the thinnest of margins, the opponent(s) may call for a fifth round beyond the standard four, called a **"whiner's round,"** to determine who "really" is the better player or team. A whiner's round has a minimum initial meld requirement of 180 points. If the issue still remains unresolved after a whiner's round, another round called a **"double whiner's round"** may also be played. A double whiner's round has a minimum initial meld requirement of 210 points.

Hand & Foot Tournament Score Sheet

This is a bit more elaborate than Hand & Foot players would use for an informal game, but it helps to track math errors and to keep tournament statistics:

Player Name				
Round #1				
Perfect Cut				
Going Out				
Total for Books				
Card Count				
Round #1 Total				
Round #2				
Perfect Cut				
Going Out				
Total for Books				
Card Count				
Round #2 Total				
Round #1 Total				
Cumulative				
Round #3				
Perfect Cut				
Going Out				
Total for Books				
Card Count				
Round #3 Total				
Prev. Cumulative				
Cumulative				
Round #4				
Perfect Cut				
Going Out				
Total for Books				
Card Count				
Round #4 Total				
Prev. Cumulative				
Final Score				

Beginners' Reference Card

To help beginning playings remember card values and bonus points, it helps to generate for them a quick reference card or sheet that looks something like the following:

Card Values:

Joker	50	
A & 2	20	
8 – K	10	
4 – 7	5	
Black 3	-5	
Red 3	-500	

Jokers & 2's wild

Bonus Points:

Perfect Cut	100
Going Out	100
Natural Book	500
Dirty Book	300

Initial Melds:

1st Round	60
2nd Round	90
3rd Round	120
4th Round	150